'Rollerblades are fast!' said Ben.
'I know,' said Rocky, 'but I like skates.'

'Can I have some rollerblades, Dad?' asked Ben.
'When you have saved up half the money,' said his Dad, 'I will give you the other half.'

Over the days that followed, Ben saved up.
He wanted to get the rollerblades.
He sold his old skates to Rocky.
Rocky was happy.

Ben saw Tony and Tessa on rollerblades in Wellington Square.
Tony was going fast.

Tony went around the statue.
He was not looking.

He ran into Mr Belter!

Mr Belter was not hurt, but he was cross.
'Tony, you were going too fast!'
said Mr Belter.

Tony was not hurt, but his rollerblades were broken.

Some days later, Ben looked out of his window.
He saw Tony and Tessa on rollerblades in Wellington Square.
He saw Rocky on his old skates.

Ben was not happy.
He did not have half the money for rollerblades.
Now he did not have his old skates.

Ben saw that Tony had new rollerblades.
They were red.
His old rollerblades were yellow.

Ben went outside into Wellington Square.
'Tony!' he shouted. 'Tony!'
Tony came over to Ben.

'What did you do with your old rollerblades?' asked Ben.
'They are broken. I could not fix the rollerblades,' said Tony.
'You can have my old rollerblades if you like.'
'Yes!' said Ben.

Ben took the broken rollerblades to his Dad.
'Can you fix the rollerblades?' Ben asked.
'I will have a go,' said his Dad.

His Dad did fix the rollerblades.
They looked like new!

Ben still had his money.
He bought the other stuff to go with the rollerblades.
He went out with his friends in Wellington Square.